WHAT I HATED MOST; PRAYING IN OTHER TONGUES!

THE SAME I AM WRITING:

BAPTISM BY FIRE.

ACTS 2:1-4.

Author: ARCHBISHOP DR MARK KAMBALAZAZA.

The truth shall set you free series.

TABLE OF CONTENTS

Foreword.

Introduction.

Chapter 1

Tongues are a direct communication with God.

Chapter 2

Tongues are for your spiritual edification.

Chapter 3

Tongues are for a human spirit's ultimate prayer

Chapter 4

Tongues are a sign to non-believers.

Chapter 5

Tongues are a sign of being rooted in Jesus Christ.

Chapter 6

Tongues can replace evil habits and addictions.

Chapter 7

Tongues are an intercession of the Holy Spirit in you.

Chapter 8

Tongues build up your most holy faith.

Chapter 9

Tongues can destroy poison, what more with HIV?

Chapter 10

Tongues are used to fight spiritual battles.

Chapter 11

Tongues are for divine interpretation to you and others.

Chapter 12

Tongues are a sign and spiritual law in Jesus' Living Church.

Chapter 13

Thirteen common satanic lies about tongues.

Conclusion.

FOREWORD.

This book is dedicated to all sons and daughters of God who seek the wisdom of God, the understanding of the baptism of the Holy Spirit, and especially the knowledge of the gift of tongues, which has confused other people for centuries. Before sharing about this gift, I will introduce the question, **"Who is the Holy Spirit?"**

There have been great testimonies from the local language readers who have read this book in the Malawi vernacular, Chewa print. They have been edified, to the extent of being baptized in the Holy Ghost on their own, praying in tongues, soon after reading the book or while reading it. I believe your testimony is coming too after reading this book.

All believers already baptized with the Holy Spirit but never understood deeply how important it is to pray in tongues will also be greatly enriched and encouraged. You will build up your faith with God-given revelations to you by the Spirit as you read this book. You will stand on top of your feet with great victory in Jesus' Name.

Satan has despised this gift of tongues for centuries. Moreover, non-believers have mocked it but due to the worldwide spiritual awakening people who love Jesus want to know more about the gift disregarding who they are and where they pray. For God is the Father of all.

May God bless my wife, Pastor Irene, Joshua, and Mark Jnr, for the support they give me.

I thank the Apostles and Bishops who made proof reading. I also thank Mr. Simbi, for their copy proof reading.

Note: Bible readings come from NIV and KJV

Introduction

I am writing this book in confession because the very same things I hated most, I am writing of them today. I hated all people who prayed in tongues. I despised them and called them mad and confused in spirit. I was very ignorant of these spiritual manifestations and gifting because of my religious doctrinal background and total ignorance of such biblical experiences. Ignorance causes many unnecessary arguments.

Yet I was sick for eleven years, from 1980 to 1991. During this time, I opposed and challenged those who were filled with the Holy Spirit. I would never mix myself with them at all for fear of spiritual contamination. However, of the same, I do write here. God, I thank you for your unending mercy and forgiveness.

Before I accepted Jesus as my Personal Lord and Savior, in my room while almost dead in the seminary, I never had any living relationship with the Holy Spirit. That is why; I despised anybody who prayed in tongues. God, I thank you for your Revelation and for sending us Jesus as our Personal Lord and Savior.

Now if you want to enjoy and understand this book, you are free now or later on to recite the life-changing prayer, I recited in 1991 on my death chamber that made me healed by Jesus.

Read aloud this prayer with me;

"Lord Jesus I surrender my life to you. I repent of all my sins and believe that you died and rose again to save me on the cross. Today I believe and receive you in my heart as my Personal Lord and Savior. I am born again, old things have now passed away and new things have come. Thank you Jesus, for coming into my life today. Now my name is written in the book of life. Father, now fill me with the Holy Spirit that I may understand what I read, in Jesus' Name. Amen!"

Now I believe that your name is written in the book of life. You have become the son or daughter of God. See **Jon 1:1-13, Rom 10:8-13**. You are a new creation. **2 Co. 5:17.**

Yes, you may decide to accept Jesus without being baptized with the Holy Spirit. You can still make it to heaven, if you obey Jesus and do his word but then you may miss a lot of the divine power ushered by the Holy Spirit. You may also miss other spiritual gifts and many spiritual victories in the life of your faith walk. That is why Jesus commanded apostles never to minister before the Holy Ghost baptism. Remember Jesus is wiser than we all are. Jesus is wiser than us to give this command

*Now let us begin with the simple question, **who the Holy Spirit is?***

WHO IS THE HOLY SPIRIT?

The Holy Spirit is not an It, no, but a real Person. He is not a dove, fire, wind, or just power as others have imagined. The Holy Spirit is a Living Person. That is why the Lord Jesus called Him, the Truth, Teacher, Him, Reminder, Testifier of Jesus Himself, He convicts the world of sin, He guides into all truth, He is the Spokesman of God, the One who glorifies Jesus, etc. See **John chapters 14 to 16.**

Let us read **Rom. 8:26-27.**

v26, "In the same way the Spirit <u>helps</u> us in our weakness. We do not know what we ought to pray for, but the Spirit <u>Himself</u> intercedes for us with groans that words cannot express v27. And he who searches our *hearts knows <u>the mind</u> of the Spirit, because the Spirit <u>intercedes</u> for the saints in accordance with God's will."*

From this passage, we read more about the Holy Spirit's personality characters, and his acts like the pronoun, **himself,** and having the **mind,** His acts include; **helping,** and **interceding** for you and me. If the Holy Spirit were fire, wind, mere power, and water, then he would not intercede for us. An intercessor is a person, not a thing. You can get help and assistance from another person, after sharing with him or her, what you have in your mind. Secondly, non-living things and animals in general cannot qualify the pronoun himself. Pronoun himself, comedy a living person. In addition, every person has a living mind for reasoning, planning, and vision. That is why the Holy Spirit intercedes for us. An "it", cannot pray for you at all. Therefore, **stop calling the Holy Spirit an "it or something told me."** He is neither an "it" nor "something (Chewa, china chake)". He is a Person, hence Him or Someone.

The Holy Spirit is a living Person because it is written he helps us in our weaknesses or infirmities; he has the mind and prays on our behalf in his intercession. Hence, the Holy Spirit, as any Person, has a spirit body and can feel, sense, hear and talk. But, he loves interceding in tongues to the father on our behalf. He indwells in you after the baptism of the Holy Ghost.

I therefore invite you to feel and to talk to the Holy Spirit, welcoming Him as you do with Jesus in your day-to-day activities for excellence. You cannot preach or minister without His help. He came for you and me. Involve Him in your daily walk life and ministry.

In Matt 28:19, Jesus qualifies the Holy Spirit as an eternal member of the Godhead.

WHY ARE MANY PEOPLE INTERESTED IN THE WORKS OF THE HOLY SPIRIT TODAY?

You know what? God has its program he carries which includes. One of these with God promised that towards the end of the world, He would pour out the Holy Spirit on everyone see *Joel 2:28* and *Acts 1:4-8, 2:1-20*. I do hope that today, you are not being left behind by this remarkable prophecy promise. God has not changed, if He did it since he began this program on Pentecost Day He is doing it, the same way today and now. Are you included or not?

Today satanic and demonic forces and oppressions like financial disasters, witchcraft, deaths, incurable satanic diseases, like HIV, and others like, bird flue, Ebola, satanic worship, prayerlessness, abounding evil, unfaithful marriages, unruly children, crime, lawlessness, etc, are all oppressions that challenge many people leaving them searching for more power, solution and answers even from God. Children of God are seeking deliverance, which Jesus gave on the cross.

Nevertheless, because the events of redemption on the cross already took place and all things prophesied were fulfilled and done, it only takes the Holy Spirit to reactivate and realize the power of the cross and bring results to you. The Holy Spirit can transfer the power of the healing wounds of Jesus to heal you today and now. The Holy Spirit activates the blood of Jesus to wash your sins away when you repent. God can only communicate to you through the help of the Holy Spirit. You cannot even see a vision of an angel without the help of the Holy Spirit.

Therefore it is spiritually suicidal to reject and deny purposely the works of the Holy Spirit. Jesus said that those who sin against the Holy Spirit will not be forgiven, in this age or in the age to come. See **Matt 12:30-32.**

I do not seek to discuss in detail who the Holy Spirit is and what all his gifts are. I have only taken one gift of the Holy Spirit, which is the most misunderstood and I want to talk deeper about the gift of tongues as the bible has written about it.

However, the Holy Spirit Baptism in the bible comes always through the manifestation of power and tongues. That is why Simon the magician wanted to buy that power from Peter in **Acts 8:18-25**. In addition, when we read the following chapters, **Act 2:1-4, 10:44-48** and **19:1-7**, we hear about the biblical initial gift of tongues and its manifestations during the Baptism of the Holy Spirit for the first 300 years of the Christian faith.

Praying in tongues in all these biblical chapters was never just a memorial of Pentecost Day but a reality of re-living the Pentecostal experience. Moreover, God never changes at all. What He did yesterday He can do today. Now if there are changes today who has done it? It is our fault and not God. Our traditions and unbiblical doctrines have removed away some spiritual roots and experiences with God.

Come Holy Spirit come quickly and join us before Jesus comes in glory.

PENTECOSTAL AND ROMAN CATHOLIC DOCTRINE; ON THE GIFT OF TONGUES.

The baptism of the Holy Spirit and the gift of tongues gradually disappeared after the 4th Century when Christianity became by order an imperial religion without genuine, necessary repentance and conversion of saints. Many became Christians by the law of Emperor Augustine without persecution of saints ended! and were born again in Rome. All the same, God was in control even as of now. This went on to the period called the Dark Ages of the Catholic Church 700 – 1500AD When witches were burnt alive and the bible was hidden from the public except for the very few high-ranking hierarchy of the church had it, written in a very difficult language called Latin. Because faith became by force an emperor's religion without believing the gospel of Jesus, the authenticity of the Holy Ghost was no longer relevant in the general sense. In a particular sense, the Lord still moved as we were served by particular saints of God throughout the Catholic Church's history.

However, through the spiritual renewal today, the baptism of the Holy Spirit has come back through the Pentecostal Movement, Catholic, and Charismatic Renewal, in the catholic and other nations, where this movement is allowed.

The doctrine of the Catholic Church accepted spiritual gifts slowly through 1964-1965 at a meeting called II Vatican Council and its documented books of the council. But about Spiritual Gifts, the church put in writing in 1987. **See "German Catechism, the Church's Confession of Faith," a Catholic Catechism for Adults, Chapters 3 and 4 on pages, 185, and 228-229.** In these pages, the gift of tongues has been described as one of the extra-ordinary gifts of the Holy Spirit among others ordinary. In this book, the church authorities have been advised not to hinder these extra-ordinary gifts but to retain and promote all that the Holy Spirit has given and is doing including the gift of tongues. It is said we must encourage and build up those who have the gifts of unity and love while respecting the established offices at the same time and vice-versa.

The 2000 AD Universal Catechism of the Catholic Church has similar information on this gift of tongues in **section 2003** under the subject of Grace, Sacramental, and Charismatic Grace, i.e. miracles or tongues. Therefore, when Mary the Mother of our Lord Jesus prayed in tongues, she did not go against any church doctrine. Praise God that we are back on track through the Charismatic and Pentecostal Revival today. Many Pentecostals believe in the biblical doctrine of spiritual gifts. They enjoy praying in tongues, praying for the sick casting out demons, etc as Jesus willed for all in **Mark 16:17-18.**

OTHER PENTECOSTAL CHURCH MINISTRIES

Lutheran Church was divided by Rev. Father Martin Luther in the 15th century and other churches out of the Catholic Church, long before the II Vatican Council, came out without the 1962-65 reformation on the Holy Spirit. Hence, many churches are still dry today.

But one most remarkable actions of Father Luther was to hide the Bible. This slowly led the world into revival because Martin Luther translated the bible from Latin to German and many translations came into being. Then the originality of Christianity became visible. It started on the Day of Pentecost, the day of the baptism of the Holy Ghost, the day of praying in tongues! ***Acts 2:1-4***

Moreover, thank God for the 1900 Spiritual awakening or revival that is sweeping the world today. That move from Azusa Street, U.S.A., and many more revivals have given birth to many Pentecostals and Charismatic Church Ministries today throughout the world. Many Christians are now stopping visiting witch doctors because Jesus can heal them. Séances are reduced because demons can now be cast out in Jesus' Name. People get born again and receive new life as was the case in the first 300 years of Christianity. People are now baptized in the Holy Spirit with the evidence of speaking in tongues, as was the case on Pentecost Day and beyond. Needs are being met by God. Satanic powers are being broken by the anointing of the Holy Ghost! In all these things, the bible has become the book of the people, not the chosen few. The Scriptures are well understood and facilitated by the Holy Ghost. Etc.

Now let us go to our main subject in this book. We must know what tongues are all about.

WHAT ARE TONGUES?

In Greek, it means glossolalia, an unintelligible language, not understood by mere human knowledge. Therefore, tongues are unintelligible utterances that a believer speaks when baptized in the Holy Spirit and his power. The one who baptizes is Jesus Himself as it is written in;

Matt 3:11. "He will baptize you with the Holy Spirit and with fire."

Fire means the Power of God given to you when you are baptized in the Spirit. The Holy Spirit as one Person of the Godhead, when He indwells a person, he speaks out through the believer from the belly of the heart, as is written in *Jon 7: 38*. No person understands the language of tongues according to the bible even the one who speaks cannot understand except when God has given you the gift of interpretation of tongues. *1Co. 14:13* and *Acts 2:5, 3:12.*

In *Act 2:13,* people on Pentecost Day understood nothing at all apart from noise and said that Mary, believers, and the Apostles, were drunk from heavy alcoholic content wine! Nevertheless, in **Acts 2:5** some of those who heard the apostles were each one able to hear in one's language. If it were, Romans only Romans should have heard. If it were, Greek only Greeks would hear. Because these people loved God they were indeed given the gift of interpretation of tongues. That is why they heard in their languages, each at the same time without translation from another speaker. What language was it then?

1 Co 14:2 we read, "**No man understands...**" the bible says that you cannot understand if you are a human being or man except sometimes, in part, through the gift of interpretation of tongues, *1 Co 14:13.* I am saying in part because you may pray in tongues long enough yet when the interpretation comes it is in seconds or very few words. Indeed, God made it a secret or mystery so that the devil must not hear, as it is written in *1 Co 14:2.*

However what is very impressive is the fact that when you pray long enough God can speak back to you through vision, peace of mind, assurance, laughter, joy, gift of knowledge, etc. See the conclusion, on feedback from God.

WHY DID MARY, APOSTLES, AND BELIEVERS SPEAK IN TONGUES ON PENTECOST DAY?

We read in *Luke 24:49* and *Acts 1:4-5* the command of Jesus Christ given to his Apostles. He commanded them not to leave Jerusalem unless they become filled with the Holy Spirit.

"On one occasion while he was eating with them, he gave them this command: "Do not leave Jerusalem but wait for the gift my Father promised, which you heard me speak about, for John baptized with water, but in few days you will be baptized with the Holy Spirit." Acts 1:4-5.

Jesus gave a command to his disciples because they believed in Jesus' command; they had to wait until the promise was fulfilled. Even now if you indeed love and believe in Jesus Christ, from deep down in your heart, you will always have a quest for the baptism of the Holy Spirit while those who reject the Living Jesus, cannot accept the Holy Ghost Baptism. Mary the mother of our Lord Jesus, Apostles, and believers on Pentecost Day, loved and obeyed the command of our Lord and they were all filled with the Holy

Spirit and started speaking in other tongues as the Holy Ghost gave them utterance.

When Jesus healed me from eleven years of infirmity in 1991, after I had read **Matt 4:23-25, Mk 5:25-34** and **Heb 13:8**, he commanded me to be filled with the Holy Spirit and be able to pray in tongues. It was tough because I hated tongues, the very support of my life. I began to pray in tongues on 2 January 1992. God used in those days, his servant, Br. Kayira. We almost all gave up because I was not ready for that, but as I gave up, thank God, Jesus never gave upon me. I began praying in tongues and I heard Jesus say, *"This is what I wanted you to be."*

Later on, as I read the bible, I discovered that Mary the Mother of our Lord Jesus whom I loved, also spoke in tongues!

WAS MARY THE MOTHER OF OUR LORD PRESENT ON THE DAY OF PENTECOST?

Act 1:14, "They all joined together constantly in prayer along with the women and Mary the mother of Jesus and with his brothers." NIV.

"These all continued with one accord in prayer and supplication, with the women and Mary the mother of Jesus and with his brothers." KJV

Therefore, indeed, Mary was present on the day of Pentecost waiting for the coming of the Holy Spirit and obeying the command of Jesus Christ. They all continued praying together and suddenly the Holy Spirit came on the tenth day of their prayer.

Act 2:1-4. "When the Day of Pentecost had fully come, they were all with one accord in one place. And suddenly there came a sound from heaven, as of a rushing mighty wind, and it filled the whole house where they were sitting. Then there appeared to them divided tongues, as of fire, and one sat upon each of them. <u>And they were all filled with the Holy Spirit and began to speak with other tongues,</u> as the Spirit gave them utterance.

They <u>were all filled</u> with the Holy Ghost and indeed Mary was inclusive. She was among the ALL, not one or two and thus without doubt she must have started praying in tongues. If there is a hardhearted person, she could not be the one! She was filled and began praying in tongues. She loved Jesus and was a much-loved woman. She was humble as such could not resist the word and command of Jesus.

Mary was a holy woman because she said, "Yes," to God's will. That is why Jesus was born through her and was ready for the baptism of the Holy Spirit. She was filled with the Holy Spirit and became a tongues praying woman. Why is she a holy woman? She housed the Most Holy One Jesus, in her womb for nine months, in her arms, shoulders, back, etc two years and lived with Jesus at home in one house for 30 years.

Now if the Holy One Jesus lived inside and outside her, she must be affected by that Godly sanctity. Hence she was made Holy by God; the indwelling of Jesus Christ and no wonder the Holy Spirit dwelt too in her and was a tongue-praying woman!

Unfortunately, Satan can make some people have questionable faith. They only stop believing in the sanctified without going beyond the Sanctifier. Stopping believing only in the one who was made holy, without going further to the one who makes people holy. Can God, Jesus, and the Holy Spirit dwell in you today? Today the world has lost the revelation of Jesus and is crushing. We all want to go to heaven where Mary our mother is but she believed in Jesus directly and did the will of God, received the Holy Ghost, and prayed in tongues.

Now, why did believers speak in tongues on Pentecost Day? There are several reasons why those who believe in Jesus do pray in tongues. We are going to study this gift through some biblical scanning. I have picked out what some verses of scriptures say about this gift without degrading the other eight gifts of the Holy Ghost. A lack of biblical knowledge has made a lot of people leave out this important yet unnoticeable gift of God. What you do not know, you cannot appreciate. People are destroyed, for lack of knowledge. You only believe what you know and use it for your victories in life.

This gift is not more important in public preaching ministry because no man can pick your words if you preach in your tongue. Yet it is very important to you as an individual. You are commanded not to forbid this gift of tongues in any way. See **1 Co. 14:39.** Let us now look at this important personal gift of the Holy Ghost.

THE MISUNDERSTOOD CHAPTER

1 Cor 14:1-40 is mostly misunderstood by many. A lot of errors have been made from there. I will also quote most from this chapter

Chapter 1

TONGUES;A DIRECT COMMUNICATION WITH GOD.

God made a spiritual direct communication between a human person and Himself. When you speak in tongues, it is like speaking on a cell phone to your dear one whom you do not see. There are sound waves and radiation in between you and the person you speak to. In the same way, this gift of tongues produces the same radiation and waves in the spirit world. That is why tongues scare demons, witches, and non-believers. You become spiritually connected with the Father of Light. It is an open dialogue between you and God.

1 Co. 14:2.

"For anyone who speaks in a tongue does not speak to men but to God. Indeed <u>no one</u> <u>understands</u> him, but he utters mysteries with his spirit".

When you speak in tongues you are not talking to anybody, but you directly talk to your Heavenly Father of Glory, through the Holy Spirit. No one can understand tongues, both the speaker as well as the hearer. That is why it is written, "No one understands." It is God's plan. God says that His mind, reasoning, is far from ours, as the heavens are higher than the earth so are God's ways higher than our ways. See *Is 55:8-9.*

Prophet Daniel's prayers were intercepted by demons of Persia because the language Daniel used was human language and any human language demons hear. Hence, the demons went and reported to the Devil and demons made a tent to intercept his answers from the heavens. Daniel suffered praying and fasting for 21 days until God intervened by sending an Archangel who destroyed the satanic interception. See *Dan 10*.

When God saw such satanic manipulation against believers' prayer life, He devised a new way of prayer that the devil and any creature should no longer hear and that is the gift of tongues. Yet sons of God have chosen still to converse with demons. They are denying the new way of heavenly communication. May be they want to be more intelligent than their Father is.

The Holy Spirit through you begins to transform negative spiritual mysteries of the devil against you into positive mysteries for you and mysteries of heaven begin to unfold upon your life into blessings, directives, and inspirations as you pray in tongues.

A mystery is anything you cannot grasp with your reasoning. There are things in life very difficult to explain or understand. Some are evil while others are good. God gave you tongues to deal with such situations, uttering and driving the negative mysteries out and gaining the glorious ones by the Holy Ghost. God favors you as a believer.

I remember one family had always nightmares in their house in, Ndirande Township, in Blantyre, Malawi. From time to time, they heard mysterious footsteps on their roof and the following morning they all became very sick, indeed for even a week. Soon, before getting better, these steps would come again. They called for many witchdoctors but they failed. Some of these doctors spent the whole night on the roof calling for more blankets to cover themselves from cold, but nothing changed. It was a mysterious phenomenon and continued to get very sick, the whole family.

After this family heard of my arrival in Blantyre in 1998 -1999, they came to me seeking God's help. I introduced them to Jesus and the Baptism of the Holy Spirit. Soon after Jesus baptized them with the Holy Spirit with the evidence of speaking in tongues, these mysterious witchcraft were destroyed. Moreover, here is their testimony;

"After almost one week we received Jesus and baptized in the spirit, we enjoyed peace. As we continued praising God for the victory but one day, the witch again came back on our roof, but when we heard of it, I immediately wake up my wife and she began praying in tongues loudly. The witch fell down on the roof with a big bang and rolled down to the ground. In the morning, we heard the news about a certain old man that he felt very sickly in the night and by the morning, he felt worse. Unfortunately, I went to see him and he confessed that we have greater charms than his this time! Since then he never came back again on top of our roof. We thank God and give him all the glory!" (Mr. and Mrs. Pipe).

Why should you continue suffering harassment at the mercy of the devil as if you do not have the Almighty Father? Witchcraft power is down played by the power of the Holy Spirit. When you do not pray in tongues, sometimes, you may suffer without victory the demonic attacks. Be filled with the Holy Spirit now and be on top!

Chapter 2

TONGUES;FOR SPIRITUAL EDIFICATION

The gift of the tongue is for spiritual edification. To edify means to solidify, to build up, to strengthen, to toughen up, etc. Therefore, edification is the action of being solidified and built up. Strengthen etc.

1 Corinthians 14:4 *says*

"He who speaks in a tongue edifies himself ……"

The bible says that if you pray in tongues you get yourself edified, fortified, and charged up. Hence, you can also build yourself up spiritually the more you pray in tongues. When I am tired of ministering for days, non-stop, I pray in tongues long enough to get back my strength from the Lord Jesus. This is a good secret for you! No wonder Paul prayed in tongues more than all at Corinthians! 1 Cor 14:16 Your faith too needs to be built up. Your healing and divine health need to be growing up with you. You need spiritual and physical strength. Your mind needs to be sound as well. But how can you attain all that edifying your spiritual body if you don't pray in tongues?

Many people do not pray in tongues to edify themselves hence; they become weaker and weaker in mind, spirit, and body. They are prone to spiritual harassment, and attacks in the mind spirit, and body. Many Christians even today complain of bewitchment for they are not spirit-filled. Are you the one? Build up yourself today. You as a believer or non-believer are at war against principalities of darkness. *(Ephesians 6:10-20)* Hence; stand up, edify yourself, and win the battles as you also pray in tongues, on your own. Be hot for the devil to handle you! You are a hot property of Jesus Christ!

Chapter 3

TONGUES; IS A HUMAN – SPIRIT'S ULTIMATE PRAYER

A human person has both the physical body as well as the spiritual body. The physical person prays in an ordinary language from the normal language of the human race. However, God planned that your spirit inside of you has to pray to him too. Hence, tongues are the prayers of your spirit body. God is a Spirit and those who worship Him must do so in spirit.

1 Corinthians 14:14, says

"For if I pray in a tongue, my spirit – prays, but my mind is unfruitful."

Praying in tongues is praying with your spirit body the physical mind news understanding anything. Here the believer's spirit is led into spiritual prayer when the Holy Spirit gives the utterance. The human spirit is spiritually nourished, empowered, and edified when you pray in tongues.

Memorized prayers cannot edify your spirit-body. Your spirit becomes strongly connected with the Heavenly Throne. You become more spiritually charged and sensitive to Divine Revelation. You know hidden things in your spirit-body.

In general, praying with your spirit-body opens your mind to comprehend easily the spiritual world and even the Holy Scriptures, which are tangible works of the Holy Spirit himself.

In my own experience, I have also discovered that thought distractions during prayers progressively, do become destroyed as you continue praying in spirit and read the bible.

That is again why Paul loved praying in tongues more than all of us today. God exalted him, and gave him the gift of miracles and wonders, **(Acts 19:1-12),** Paul wrote many scriptures, traveled long missionary journeys, founded many churches, etc. Though highly educated, he loved praying in tongues and God used him. Aren't you willing, to sale out you're his learning and philosophies as belief in God? Nourish your spirit man build him up and he will be very strong and you will become used to God.

Some people have starved their spirits and have been easily defeated by the enemy. The devil attacks the spirit. If your spirit does not know how to pray in tongues, it is very difficult to defend yourself and fight back. Somebody may be very fat but with a very slim spirit body if one prays not with his spirit. You may be slim in the physical body yet be powerful in spirit because of being spirit-filled and tongues praying. Charge your spirit man now and begin to exercise dominion over the devil in righteousness & holiness.

Chapter 4

TONGUES;ARE FOR A SIGN TO NON BELIEVERS.

1 Corinthians 14:22 says

"Tongues then are a sign, not for believers but for unbelievers."

Unbelievers become confused, and they want neither to talk nor to hear about it.

The bible says that those who pray in tongues do not wonder, but the unbelievers wonder much, what that noise, is all about. They joke, insult, and even mock this gift of the Holy Spirit. It is a sign of contention for non-believers. They laughed at it all and rejected it when the gift was given initially. That was what I was doing when I was spiritually ignorant.

In **Act 2:13,** on Pentecost Day the non-believers accused the Apostles and believers of having drunken wine, they laughed at them. Even if the non-believers did that, it still became a sign of conviction to them so much so that 3,000 were converted to Jesus Christ, and were baptized. Even if people laugh at you, continue to enjoy this gift, and one day through your life of testimony, they will believe, repent, and receive Christ Jesus. That is how my relatives did after they laughed at me for some time, today they are all born again.

Tongues, therefore make a clear difference between a believer who has been baptized in the Holy Spirit and a non-believer. Hence, it is not a problem for believers but for non-believers. They do not know what it is all about.

People laugh at this gift because of ignorance at its best. Others do it intentionally against the warning of Jesus Christ in **Mathew 12:30-32**, which talks about unpardonable sin if you sin against the Holy Spirit. Where are you? Are you a believer? Then be filled with the Holy Spirit a heart in Jesus' name.

Chapter 5

TONGUES;ARE A SIGN OF BEING ROOTED IN JESUS CHRIST.

Mark 16:17-18, Jesus clearly says,

"And these signs will ACCOMPANY those who believe; in my name they will drive out demons; they will speak in new tongues continue with the wise Jesus himself is telling you directly that his sign& wonder will accompany you. He cannot lie, if you don't have his sign question yourself "

Other Bibles say **that signs will follow** those who believe in Jesus, those who have rooted their faith in Jesus Christ. Tongues therefore are a sign of total commitment to Jesus Christ, total surrendering of one's whole being, mind, sound, tongue, words inclusive.

When you accept Jesus genuinely, you develop a hunger for the Holy Spirit. That is why many who receive Jesus end up being baptized in the spirit.

People are not humble, when they fail to commit their lives to Jesus Christ, those who trust in their knowledge, theologies, philosophies, and the scientific mind, cannot be filled with the Holy Spirit. In other words, Jesus says, that those who are not like him, who do not believe in him, those who are not broken-hearted his signs; tongues inclusive, cannot follow them at all. He said this for the coming generations. To avoid human pretense he said it. If you believe in Jesus tongues follow you. If you only pretend, no Jesus sign can accompany you at all. Nominal xiam cannot have signs of Jesus.

Today I see many people who claim to believe in Jesus but without any sign following them. Are you in that group? Why don't you ask Jesus Christ to manifest in you his signs of believing in him? Since Jesus commanded me to be spirit-filled in 1991, I have seen uncountable people accepting the Living Jesus with his signs and wonders following. Many have and are praying in tongues, now.

Chapter 6

TONGUES;CAN REPLACE EVIL HABITS AND ADDICTIONS

Ephesians 5:18 says tongues can replace ………………………

"Do not get drunk on wine, which leads to debauchery. Instead, be filled with the Spirit"

Drinking beer leads you to other evil habits. The bible commands you to be filled with the Spirit to avoid destruction with liquor and other evil habits. However, constant renewal and repeatedly being filled with the Holy Spirit automatically and progressively drive away all evil habits. The more you become friendly with the Holy Spirit, the more He directs you and leads you into a holy life. The Spirit replaces the evil behavior. Moreover, when you maintain the living faith in Jesus Christ, you automatically have a thirst for more infilling of the Spirit, praying in psalms of praise and in tongues. That slowly changes your life. You discover that things like music, novels, movies, liquor addiction, etc begin to bore you very much. You automatically begin to love things of God. You begin to enjoy reading the bible and love praying.

By experience, I have seen many people, who love praying in tongues, who are led by the Holy Spirit, and who love Jesus, change for the better and you see a holy godly life in them. Hence, get ready for the transformation of your likes in life. Evil habits will disappear and you will see it.

Jesus commanded his Apostles not to leave Jerusalem unless they were filled with the Holy Spirit in **Acts 1:4-5.** They obeyed Jesus' command and after being filled they began praying in tongues (Acts **2:1-4),** they were liberated from the power of fear that led Peter to deny Jesus. Shame also disappeared. They became bold and testified Jesus unto death to the amazement of thousands of people. You will surprise many people soon! Therefore, you cannot deny saying that there is power to destroy fear, shame, and other evil inclinations in the baptism of the Holy Spirit.

What evil habits are ruining your life? Why don't you replace them with the indwelling of the Holy Spirit? He is the Spirit called Holy, meaning, Sanctifier, Purifier. Be holy and live for God. Time is running out.

Chapter 7

TONGUES;IS AN INTERCESSION OF THE HOLY SPIRIT IN YOU

You may have many problems in your life. Some of them you do not even know where they come from. Often you even fail to express yourself for an answered prayer before God. No Heavenly reply comes to you. Your language runs short of words to talk to God for a break through. Sometimes you only give up as a solution. But God loves you so much that he gave a solution to all that.

In **Romans 8:26-27** we read,

"In the same way the Spirit helps us in our weakness. We do not know what we ought to pray for, but the Spirit himself "intercedes for us" with groans that words cannot express. And he, who searches our hearts, knows the mind of the Spirit, because the Spirit intercedes for the saints in accordance with God's will"

The Holy Spirit came with tongues to help you in any of your possible weaknesses. He came to lift you up, to support you day and night. More to it, he supports you in your prayer life. He knows how to talk to God better than you do. Hence, the Holy Spirit has to make intercession for you to God directly through these wonderful groans, not expressible in your own natural words. Why? It is because your human language is too weak to express yourself fully before God. You may give another meaning of this phrase, "groans, that words cannot express." Bu no matter what other meanings you give, I add to it, groanings, as also the gift of tongues because I believe that tongues are a part of the groans of the Holy Spirit. Remember 1 Corinthian 14:2, that tongues are not an ordinary earthly language. Nevertheless, it is that which, "Words cannot express."

When you pray in tongues, God hears what the Holy Spirit is saying in you, on your behalf. He intercedes for you, saint of God, directly to your Father without error. It is always in the will of God. Sometimes when you pray in tongues long enough you can have feedback from heaven. often it is an instruction on what to do, to have a break through. Why don't you take on this Divine advantage of being prayed for by the Holy Spirit? Rise up for the gift of faith by the power of the Holy Spirit. Personally, I have seen the Holy Spirit doing a lot of prayer for me, and have experienced break through, direction, and instruction from God. After taking such instruction from above, I have seen great things happen.

Chapter 8

TONGUES; BUILD UP YOUR MOST HOLY FAITH

Everyone born of God craves to have one's faith grow. The more your faith grows, the more spiritual maturity and victories come by. When you don't grow in faith, you cannot command influence in the Spirit world. The Bible says that you can't please God if you don't have faith, **Hebrews 11:6.** Actually when your faith grows, problems simply become opportunities to see more of God's power and dominion.

The bible speaks of some ways to build up faith and tongues or praying in the spirit is one other way.

Jude 20 says

"But you, dear friends, build yourselves up in most holy faith and pray in the Holy Spirit," (NIV). But RSV does not have "and". It simply says pray in the Holy Spirit. Here it means that praying in the Holy Spirit (tongues) will help you to build up your faith.

According to experience, when one becomes just baptized in spirit, with the evidence of speaking in tongues, the faith becomes indeed stimulated. I have seen many people shedding tears of Joy, while others see powerful visions of Jesus, Angels, Heaven, etc. You indeed begin to live in the spirit more than in the natural. It is indeed an enjoyable experience but unfortunately, some do not continue with speaking in tongues, but abandon it all. Live in it and continue to enjoy such experiences and stimulate your faith. Praying in tongues will cause your faith to grow and your love for Jesus will grow too. Faith is a spiritual gift and among other things, the Holy Spirit enables our spiritual man to increase faith. Every person who prays in tongues has an automatic thirst for the word of God, which continues to make faith grow. **Rom 10:17**

The world as it is now needs men and women of faith to subdue it, to put the enemies of our God under the feet of Jesus before his second coming.

Be filled with the Holy Spirit now in Jesus name!!

Chapter 9

TONGUES; CAN DESTROY POISON; WHAT MORE WITH HIV?

If tongues can destroy poison, according to the teachings of Jesus below, then it goes without mentioning that sickness and diseases can also be destroyed. You know for sure that poison is more deadly than HIV microorganisms. I believe that if tongues destroy poison, which is the most dangerous substance to the body, then viruses and bacteria if they are foreign to the body can easily and in the same way be eradicated. How can tongues destroy poison as well as viruses and bacteria? Let us read what Jesus has said.

New Int Version says;

"And these signs will accompany those who believe: In my name they will drive out demons; they will speak in new tongues; they will pick up snakes with their hands; and when they drink deadly poison, it will not hurt them at all; they will place their hands on sick people, and they will get well."

KIV says signs should fellow. In this chapter, Jesus says that his signs and wonders will, automatically follow believers. Rather when the Living Jesus is in you, heavenly signs begin to follow you because the King Himself is in you, the owner of signs and wonders is dwelling inside of you and you flow in the anointing of the Holy Spirit. Therefore, this means that if Jesus is not in you or you pretend to have Jesus, yet you do not have him, no signs will follow you. You cannot cast out demons but demons can cast you out instead. You can laugh at people who pray in tongues because that would not make sense to you.

Casting out demons is number one then comes speaking in new tongues, thirdly is dissolving any snake or deadly poison, the more you pray in tongues. Jesus says that it will not hurt you at all. I personally believe that accident and not mere deliberate drinking of it in liters must do the taking in of poison. I was given poison unawares, in 1998, October; I survived that attack even after eating half the fish that contained deadly poison. Instead, the one who did it died sometime later. When God told me that I had taken poison He directed me to pray in tongues until everything was flushed out by God's promise and power of the Holy Ghost! If I were not filled with the Holy Spirit and never knew how to pray in tongues, I would be dead by then.

Jesus cannot cheat us because lies only belong to the devil. Search and receive from Him and from what he is saying to you.

Now let us take another biblical tangible truth. In 1 Corinthians 14:18, Paul told us that he prayed in tongues more than all the Corinthians. Acts 28:1-4; a poisonous and deadly snake bit him. Nothing happened, no swelling, no dying. Make the connection yourself on this.

After praying for my nephew in 1992 at home, he received Jesus as his Personal Lord and Savior and he was filled with the Holy Spirit and began praying in tongues. After some time, a poisonous snake bit him. He rushed into my house and prayed in tongues for not less than twenty minutes. He heard inside of him the word, "Over!" Nothing hurt him until today. In Zomba the wife of the Charismatic Pastor, had the same experience, snakebite, yet she was not again harmed. Our God is not an ordinary one. What about your God? We have an extraordinary God, full of power and Miracles.

Now my question is, what is more deadly, between poisons, be it a snakebite or liquid poison and HIV? Between HIV and poison, which brings instant killing more than the other does? It is of course poison. Yet when you pray in tongues, poison, the deadly thing does not work at all. What about the lesser? Then it goes without mentioning that when you believe in Jesus and are Spirit praying in tongues constantly then, any body poisoning, HIV inclusive cannot harm you. Through the power of Jesus and praying in tongues with the power of the word I have seen many people being set free and you can dissolve HIV as you can do so with poison if you pray in tongues constantly. What matters here is not presumption but faith in the Living Jesus, which is followed by the signs and wonders, mentioned above.

Doctor Jesus already lives inside of you what is your problem? I commanded demons of HIV, body poison to leave you in Jesus' name.

Tongues generate the healing anointing which enables us to dissolve poison. When you read the bible you won't hear the tongue-powerful speaker Paul dying of plagues, sickness, and infirmity. He was martyred in Rome. You can therefore drive out the virus of aids if you are serious. I have seen this happening. Again You cannot please God without faith. If Paul survived a deadly poisonous snake, with the same Jesus and Spirit, with the same God, why can't you survive today? Remember with faith all things are possible before you.

The same God, who is healing today and who healed me from eleven years of affliction, from 1980 to 1991 can heal you even now! After Jesus healed me in 1991, he ordered me to receive the Holy ghost and begin praying in tongues in 1991. On 2nd Jan 1992, it happened. I bless God for the Divine health he gave me and placed on my life in that year. It is my prayer now that God places on you His divine life so that you enjoy his health and benefits as you follow his purposes! May our God be glorified forever in Jesus name.

Chapter 10

TONGUES; ARE USED TO FIGHT SPIRITUAL BATTLES

When you begin to pray in tongues, the Spirit world of the devil becomes disturbed indeed. If praying in tongues is talking directly to God (1 Corinthians 14:2) then all atmospheric evil spirits or spirits of the air most become confused because they cannot understand whatever is going to happen between you and God. The demons do not know what comes next. Because any Divine revelation as it may come by through the gift of tongues can destroy their plans.

Remember how Daniel was intercepted in **Daniel 10**, as he spoke to God in ordinary language, the reporting demon heard him and went to accuse him of his master the devil. Daniel was blocked for 21 days. When the angel of God came to Daniel, he reported that God heard him the first day he prayed but the prince of Persia blocked him on the way for 21 days. Demons hear every language you speak. They have overstayed here on earth and they are more experienced than you are. Yet even though God devised a new way of communicating with Him above Satan, many still do not want to enjoy the privilege God has given. What else should God do?

In *Ephesians 6:10-20* we read;

"Finally, be strong in the Lord and in his mighty power. Put on the full armour of God, so that you can take your stand against the devil's schemes …………. For our struggle is not against flesh and blood but against the rulers, against the authorities ……… powers of this dark world ……. Against spiritual forces of evil in the heavenly realms (places), stand firm then …….. verse 18 ……… <u>pray in the spirit</u> with all kinds of prayer and request".

Here tongues are inclusive in praying in the spirit with all kinds of prayers.

In this chapter, you can use the gift of tongues for your spiritual battles and victories. *In Luke 24:49,* Jesus talked about that power. I Acts 1:8; Jesus told the Apostles that after the baptism in the Holt Spirit, They would receive power to witness Jesus with signs and wonders. The same power You have been given this power if you pray in tongues. Know it, believe it, pray in tongues use it, and see the results. Time to suffer ongoing satanic manipulation is over and it is over for you. You are free when you know the truth. Victory is yours in Jesus' name. I see somebody enjoy his and her freedom now in Jesus' Name. I believe it is you. What Daniel could not do in the Old Testament you can now do today. Use tongues and the anointing to fight the enemy and win now! Be filled with the Holy host now in Jesus name.

Chapter 11

TONGUES;

ARE FOR DIVINE INTERPRETATION TO YOU AND OTHERS

The other advantage of praying in tongues is that God can tell you straight what he wants you to do, or others to do through the gift of interpretation of tongues. You can consult God on several issues and receive Divine revelations through this gift. You can know hidden things. When you express yourself to God what you want and you involve the Holy Spirit to intercede for you in tongues after some time you hear an interpretation "if you ask" for it. I have managed to receive a lot of information through this gift of tongues.

You can ask God easily using the gift of tongues

1 Corinthians 14:13 says

"For this reason anyone who speaks in a tongue should pray(or ask God) that he may interpret what he says".

You can ask God to interpret for you as you start praying in tongues. However, some people cannot receive the interpretation because of two things. First, they do not ask God for the interpretation as they begin praying in tongues. Secondly, they do not pray long enough while expecting the interpretation to come. We are in a fast world. Do not be in a hurry with God. Timing must belong to God alone. Yours is praying and expectation in faith. Now, how do you know the actual interpretation?

An interpretation comes out of your mouth when the tongues suddenly cease and English or your local language automatically is spoken. You experience an automatic switching your the tongue. Your mind registers up your language as you pray in tongues. Sometimes the words are constantly repeated in your language as they come out of your mouth. Interpretation comes also in your mind, but in the same way. It is like a new thought pattern coming now and again.

The Holy Spirit is able also to reveal to you the need to pray for others by mentioning their names. I have read a book by Brother Kenneth Hagin. He saved his dying brother through the revelation of his brother's name by the Holy Spirit as he prayed in tongues. It was testified on the following day.

In 2002, January as I was praying in tongues in Blantyre I heard an interpretation to pray for a certain woman in Lilongwe. Her name came to my tongue several times. I prayed for her indeed and God saved her from the demonic trap. It was confirmed when I called for her in 2002 January in Lilongwe.

Let us cover one another with what God has given us. Now in the following chapter you are about to read, you may have read in the papers or heard others who have spoken negatively about the gift of tongues. The devil is a liar and he is still cheating many today after he cheated Adam and Eve. He has not stopped his schemes. Let us examine some of these lies from the pit of hell. Let us see some lies of the devil against the gift of tongues.

Chapter 12

THIRTEEN COMMON SATANIC LIES ABOUT TONGUES.

1. Tongues are but a gift only to the favorites!

This is a lie because in **Joel 2:28** God says that the Holy Ghost would be poured on all peoples. Secondly, Jesus commanded **all** apostles to wait for the Holy Ghost and they were **all** filled and **all** began to pray in other tongues as the Spirit enabled **them** to speak. There were 120 people in all on this day. See **Acts 1:4-8** and **2:1-4**. At Cornelius' family, they **all** prayed in tongues. **Acts 10:44-48.** The Lord Jesus said that the Father would never deny anybody who asks of the Holy Ghost from Him in **Luke 11:11-13**.

2. Tongues are for the Pentecostal Christians only.

This is another lie because Jesus said that tongues would follow all people who believe in Him, according to **Mk 16:17-18**. *"And these signs will follow those who believe: In My name, they will cast out demons: they will speak with new tongues...."*

So tongues are not for Pentecostals alone but all who claim to believe in Jesus, all who call themselves Christians or Christ-like but in truth. Jesus never said that these signs would follow the Pentecostals but those who believe! If you believe in Jesus no matter what your denomination is, you qualify.

3. Tongues are lies of misinformed believers.

Jesus cannot misinform anybody. The devil misinforms you. Some Christian traditions have indeed a lot of misinformation about other biblical truths. Jesus never misinformed his disciples when he commanded never to move but to wait for the Holy Spirit in Acts 1:4-5; 8. They obeyed and filled with the Holy Ghost and prayed in tongues. **Acts 2:1-4.** Mary was even there on Pentecost Day, **Acts 1:14.** Therefore, she must have also prayed in tongues. I do not believe she was misinformed when she prayed in tongues. Doctrinal errors have misinformed people indeed. Sometimes what I do not understand as a leader can reflect in others by my authority in ignorance. Hence, we must continue to seek the Lord. I said that it was exactly what I believed after. I dint know that it was my lack of knowledge against tongues speaking to cover-up others and myself in ignorance. When I knew, I repented to God.

4. Tongues were only for the first church.

This is another lie from the pit of hell. The gift of the Holy Ghost is for you and even your children to come. ***Acts 2:38-39, "Repent and let every one of you be baptized in the name of Jesus Christ for the remission of sins; and you shall receive the gift of the Holy Spirit. For the promise is to you and to your children, and all who are afar off as many as the Lord our God will call."***

Therefore, this gift is for all today and even those whom God shall call in the future, far and beyond. Hence, it is an unending gift from the start to the future. Therefore, we are saying that it is not true to say that tongues were for the first church.

5. Tongues come when you have prayed a lot.

Tongues come when you are filled with the Holy Ghost not when you have prayed a lot. You are not a diesel maize mill to start praying in tongues by pulling the mill handle several times before it starts grinding.

Acts 10:44-48, "While Peter was still speaking these words, the Holy Spirit came on all who heard the message. The circumcised believers who had come with Peter were astonished that the gift of the Holy Spirit had been poured out even on the Gentiles. For they heard them speaking in tongues and praising God."

Here the Holy Spirit filled the people and began to pray in tongues as Peter was preaching to them not because people were praying, not at all. But as they were hearing the Gospel truth from Peter they were all filled with the Spirit. So do not limit the Holy Spirit. He can come on you even as you read this book! It has happened to many readers who have testified, after reading the local vernacular translation of this book. Be able to pray with ease in tongues.

6. Tongues were forbidden by Paul.

This lie comes to you when you have not read all, *1 Co. 14:1-40*. Many have misunderstood Paul by reading this chapter in part. In that case, Paul said that,

"Therefore' my brothers, be eager to prophesy, and do not forbid speaking in tongues. But everything should be done in a fitting and orderly way." 1 Co.14:39-40.

Paul never forbade you from praying in tongues because he cannot oppose his own Master, Jesus who said tongues would follow you if you believe in Him, **Mk 16:17-20.** But if you don't believe in Jesus why should the gift of the Holy Ghost come on you? Even tongues would be a nuisance because He who sent the Holy Spirit is not in you.

7. Tongues are demonic manifestations.

Apostles, believers, and Mary the Mother of our Lord Jesus, were not filled with demons on Pentecost Day but with the Holy Ghost as they prayed in tongues. *Acts 2:1-4.*

At Ephesus, Paul went to preach the Gospel.

"When Paul placed his hands on them, the Holy Spirit came on them and they spoke in tongues and prophesied. There were about twelve men in all." Act 19:1-7

The Spirit came not demons came. If Jesus is in you, you cannot pray to him and receive demons. If you are a Satanist yes then demons can fill you the more but if you believe Jesus, He is faithful to honor your request and not send you demons. See *Luke 11:11-13.*

8. Tongues are meaningless and useless.

1 Co. 14:2, "For anyone who speaks in a tongue does not speak to men but God. Indeed, no one understands him; he utters mysteries with his spirit."

Speaking to the Father is not useless rather it is meaningful to Him and beneficial to you. Even though, you do not understand what you are saying, God understands what the Holy Spirit is saying for you on your behalf. It is you, who benefits a lot and God can give interpretation to you. As you pray, you are talking mysteries in the spirit, you are destroying whatever, Satan intended to do in your life, which is always a mystery. When the church is full of witches and people who don't know the word of God, it is very difficult to accept the move of the Holy Ghost! Tongues are God's secrete language between you and him and it is not true to say that, tongues are meaningless.

Tongues are one of the nine gifts of the Holy Spirit. God cannot give a meaningless gift to his own sons and daughters. Do not make my God meaningless God. He is ever meaningful and whoever obeys Him enjoys life in its fullness. *John 10:10.*

9. Tongues bring confusion in the church.

Indeed, it brings confusion in the church when elders and pastors want to preach in tongues and always pray in tongues instead of ordinary language for others to hear and say amen! That is what Paul is talking about in *1 Co. 14.* Yet Paul himself prayed in tongues more than anybody did. *Verse 18-19.* However, in the church, he would like to preach in ordinary language so that sinners may repent and receive Jesus as their personal Lord and Savior.

Paul in this chapter 14 ends up by saying that do not you dare forbid praying in tongues.

Again, when Jesus said that tongues would follow those who believe he never meant that confusion would follow. Not at all! However, the use of any gift if it is not well understood can bring confusion. Even the gift of prophecy itself and its ministry if not well understood could bring confusion. Jesus did not bring gifts of the Holy Spirit to confuse. Yes but speaking in tongues before the devil, indeed becomes confused because he does not understand. God confused him.

10. Not all can pray in tongues.

For some time I personally believed in this lie. However, since the Lord Jesus gave me the gift of the baptism of the Holy Ghost, I have witnessed that all who requested and desired this gift receive it. My mother in 1992 could not pray in tongues the first time we prayed. I asked the Lord why. It was because she could not forgive in her spirit. When we prayed the third time after she forgave all, she prayed in tongues and later on vomited a lot of blood. Unforgiveness, worries, hatred and bitterness, lack of understanding about the ministry of the Spirit, unbelief, etc have indeed been hindering others from being baptized in the Spirit.

"But if you do not forgive, neither will your Father in heaven forgive your trespasses." Mk 11:26.

God is love without it, it is difficult for the Holy Spirit to dwell in you. Jesus said that all could be given the Holy Spirit if they ask and God cannot deny anybody if one asks from Him. see **Luke 11:11-13.** I testify that even those who have come to me and said that they have never succeeded in praying in tongues have prayed in tongues in my presence. God is no respecter of persons. He cannot allow some to speak to Him and ban others from speaking to Him. Others who have had higher education, like philosophy, can bind their mind to the freedom of the Spirit. That too was my problem.

11. <u>Tongues are a gift given to some.</u>

Please understand carefully what the Spirit is saying here. Yes, tongues are a gift, according to *1 Co. 12:8-10*, but again it **is above being a mere gift**. The difference lies from *1 Co.12: 4-6,* between the baptism of the Holy Ghost as a gift **and** the actual praying in tongues itself. Not all who pray in tongues can pray for others to become baptized in the Holy Spirit to others, also and pray in tongues.

Phillip who preached in Samaria with mighty signs and wonders, *(Acts 8),* called for Apostle Peter, who had the ministry gift of baptism of the Holy Spirit, and John accompanied Peter, yet all, Philip inclusive had the gift of tongues. When Peter came, there was a great demonstration of the Spirit, which even Simon the magician wanted to buy with money. However, Peter rebuked him, and the witch repented. You have power above witches when you are baptized in the Spirit; you are above witches and magicians!

In this chapter of 1Cor 12, Paul combines gifts, services, or ministries and works, together as he talks about spiritual gifts. He interrelates them all. When you single out can

See *1 Co. 12:4-5*. *"There are different kinds of gifts, but the same Spirit. There are different kinds of service or (ministry) but the same Lord there are different kinds of working, but the same God works all of them in all men."*

This chapter combines, gifts, ministries, and works together with the nine gifts of the Holy Spirit. If you remove ministries and works, you cannot well understand how the gift of tongues operates. When you remove them, you indeed only remain with gift as the whole truth here. Therefore, you must combine all nine gifts with their works and ministries. You also need to go to the whole bible and search for praying in tongues separately from this chapter to have a wider understanding.

Jesus told us that tongues would follow all those who believe in Him. See Mk *16:17-20* above. Thirdly, praying in tongues according to *1 Co. 14:2*, is speaking to your Father in Heaven. It is direct communication with God. Who should stop you from believing in Jesus and communicating directly with your Father? Why should some speak to their Father while you don't speak to yours? Why should you be? God wants you to speak to Him directly. The devil is a liar!

Fourthly, in **Rom 8:26-27** tongues is an intercession of the Holy Spirit in you. The Holy Ghost makes intercession on behalf of the saints! It is with groanings, (tongues inclusive), beyond mere human words!

Therefore, praying in tongues is; One. **A sign**. Two. **A gift**. Three. **A speech to the Father** in the Spirit and, Four. **Intercession of the Spirit for you**. If you miss it as a gift, get is as a sign. If you miss it as a sign, get it as an intercession of the Spirit. If you miss it as an intercession, get it as a speech to your Dad in Heaven. You cannot miss all these divine privileges!

12. Speaking in tongues is difficult.

If you pray with your mind, it is difficult to speak in tongue for the mind wants to grasp what you are saying. If you think it is your own doing, it is hard. But if you have faith that praying in tongues is of the Holy Spirit then it is easy because you will understand that it is no longer you speaking but the Holy Spirit in you, who is speaking. If you submit your tongue, mouth, sound, and your will to Him as a Person, you can easily accept him speaking through you.

Depend on God and not on yourself. It is very easy to pray in tongues when you understand this. Your knowledge and your thinking have no part in it. Rather you will wonder what your tongue is saying because your mind does not comprehend what you are saying unless you are given the interpretation of tongues, within your mind by God as you pray.

13. True tongues are understood by all.

This is another terrible lie from the devil. He cannot understand tongues and has played many hidden games to hinder sons and daughters of God from spiritual progress and knowledge.

1 Co 14:14, "For if I pray in a tongue, my spirit prays, but my UNDERSTANDING (mind), is unfruitful."

Your understanding or your mind does not get what you are saying according to the bible. In **verse 13,** we also read, *"Therefore let him who speaks in tongues*, (or who wants to preach in tongues in the church*), pray that he may interpret."* So tongues you do not hear what you are saying unless by the gift of interpretation as the bible is saying. Leave the devil alone with his lies.

On Pentecost Day, some who feared and loved God heard each one in their own languages separately but everyone at the same time. But there was no interpretation. God did it. Yet many people said they were drunk of wine for these many people never understood anything. See **Acts 2:4-5 and 13**.

In addition, when Peter began speaking he addressed the people who accused them of wine because they must have been more than those who received divine interpretation. You do not get disturbed much and quit ministering because of one rebellious man out of a million who is following you.

Chapter 13

TONGUES; ARE AS A SIGN AND A LAW IN JESUS' LIVING CHURCH

1 Corinthians 14:38-40, "<u>If he ignores</u> this, <u>he himself will be ignored</u>. Therefore my brothers be eager to prophesy, and <u>do not forbid</u> speaking in tongues. But everything should be done in a fitting and orderly way."

The context of this chapter is that Paul was creating and giving an order of proper worship, at a certain church in Corinth. At this church, believers were even preaching in tongues in the hearing of even visitors. There was nobody who was speaking out God's message or prophesying in the ordinary language. Therefore, Paul was instilling an order of worship without forbidding people at the same time from praying in tongues. Paul could not hinder and oppose what Jesus taught from **Mk 16:17-18**, that believers would be followed by the gift of praying in tongues, among other signs.

The word of God emphasizes that preaching in tongues in the church assembly would not benefit anybody unless there were two or three people with the gift of interpretation of tongues to help others.

Therefore, Paul exalts those who preach in the ordinary language in the church more than those who would preach in tongues, yet, without castigating praying in tongues. This is proven by Paul himself who boasts of speaking in tongues more than anyone at Corinth does, even above you, if you compare yourself with him. *1 Cor. 14:18,* yet this man was the graduate of his day.

Even though prophecy is above tongues in the church assembly, the bible warns us still against forbidding people from praying in tongues in their lives;

The bible warns non-believers as well as those who believe with wrong faith and wrong focus, not to forbid anyone from praying in tongues. Nobody is above the word of God no matter his or her position in the church may be. You are commanded not to forbid anyone from praying in tongues, even forbidding yourself is not permitted.

Your focus therefore must be the Lord Jesus Christ as he is the only way to heaven, *John 14:6-7.* In addition, Jesus commanded that **sings would follow those who believe and tongues are one of those commanded signs.** See *Mark 16:17-20*. Thus, the living church of Jesus cannot do without obeying their Master. The Chief Cornerstone has said it and so nobody can oppose it. It is either you are for Him or not. Jesus, Church without any argument has therefore these signs since the day of Pentecost. He never changes but people, theories, and teachings change! If you ignore deliberately spiritual gifts God shall also ignore you, it is written. If you make tongues your refuse, God shall make you refuse too. That is what it means.

Why did Jesus command the Apostles never to minister before the descending of the Holy Spirit? Why ministry was not allowed without the baptism of the Holy Spirit? See *Acts 1:4-8* and *Luke 24:49*. The answer is that Jesus wanted the Apostles to preach and witness his Name, with power that is above the power of the devil. Moreover, as apostles obeyed this command and received the Holy Ghost, there was indeed a demonstration of the Holy Ghost's power wherever the Apostles went.

"Everyone was filled with awe, and many wonders and miraculous signs were done by the apostles." Acts 2:43.

These signs and wonders came about when they were filled with the Holy Ghost, while Jesus had ascended into Heaven. You cannot preach in your own power and expect results. You preach and people sleep!

Why then must Jesus allow you today to minister without His power if he never allowed his very own Apostles? If you ignore this gift, the only way is for you simply to be ignored according to the word from above. If I were you, I would pray to God to give me hunger and thirst for the Holy Spirit right now. I would start praying immediately and ask Jesus to fill me with the Holy Spirit. In the middle of my prayer, I would begin praying in tongues on my own with the trust that Jesus would fill my hunger with the baptism of the Holy Ghost. If I would need more help, I would go for an anointed man of God who could help me. Nevertheless, Jesus says that **God cannot deny you the infilling of the Holy Ghost.**

Why waste time? John the Baptist said, *"He will baptize you with the Holy Spirit and with fire." Matt 3:11*. I cannot wait but just ask Jesus to do it now!

Do you know that God's end-time vision must not pass over you? Do you know that you can be left out of **God's end-time vision**?

See *Joel 2:28* again. *"And afterward, I will pour out my Spirit on <u>all people</u>. Your sons and your daughters will prophesy, your old men will dream dreams, your young men will see visions. Even on my servants, both men and women, will I pour out my Spirit in those days."*

God's end-time vision includes <u>all people</u>, sons and daughters, old men and young men, even servants or slaves both men and women! Then if God includes all, why should you be left behind? Why should God leave you or why should you live yourself out? This is not a traditional church teaching but a biblical truth of Heavenly timing! It is God's end-time vision and not man's end-time vision! What wrong have you done to be left out if Mary the Mother of Jesus and Apostles obeyed why don't you also obey? Paul said who has bewitched you. May God help you!

CONCLUSION

Tongues is …….. biblical guidance of baptism in Spirit.

The Holy Spirit has nine gifts according to **1 Corinthians 12:4-10**. Nevertheless, in the book of Acts, the gift of tongues remains an open door to the other eight gifts. If you follow the biblical manifestation of the unchangeable God, you will understand it. See **Acts 2:1-4, 10:44-48** and **19:1-7**. Wherever the Apostles went to minister, the Holy Spirit came on the believers and the people began praying in tongues first more than anything else, as the Spirit gave them utterance. On Pentecost, there were tongues first, then preaching, baptism, and miracles. You cannot be confused with false doctrine if you take the simple straightforward biblical study perspective.

Become bible ……… to grow up spiritually

Secondly, as you keep on praying in tongues, your faith shall be stimulated, and even your spiritual understanding will change. You will see Jesus lively in your heart. However, you also need to stimulate spiritual growth by reading and studying the bible every day. This combination will make you grow fast in spirit and faith. You will have an impact in the spirit world and your dominion as you do the word will be unquestionable. You can pray in tongues and not grow spiritually if you do not become a student of the word. That is the whole story in **1 Corinthians 14:1-40, 2 Tim. 3:14-17 and Matt. 7:21-27.** The doers of God's word are those who have received a guarantee to become members of heaven and the redeemed of Jesus.

Study the word of God Day and night and obey it, and you will make success and prosperity follow you – see *Joshua 1:8.* When you add to it praying in tongues then you become **a spiritual nuclear reactor and bomb!** Do it and see to enjoy the results. God will lift you in your humility, obedience, and love for love is the ultimate gift of God. **However, remember the feedback!**

YOU MUST GET A FEEDBACK FROM GOD.

God has spiritual signals he gives to many people. They are but burdens, in the heart, inviting you to prayer. These signals could be in the form of a lack of peace, without your worries, a heavy burden in your heart yet without any negative thoughts. Sometimes you get a strange, chest palpitation, signaling you to pray in tongues. At night, you may feel as if someone is waking you up or sometimes taking your sleep away yet without a word. Others have an intense fear in the spirit when the Spirit sees rooming danger. If you ignore these signals, you may be attacked. All that is the Holy Spirit calling you to prayer but many miss Him and become vulnerable to demonic attacks even sudden deaths. Others have received similar and same evil dreams repeatedly calling you to cancel Satan's plans by prayer and fasting. Yet some have missed it and perished. However, He continues calling you and me with signals to prayer. Please beloved obey him.

If praying in tongues is indeed speaking to God then you must **be assured of God's feedback** to you. God indeed loves to speak back to you using different kinds of spiritual signals plus His very own word, audible to you and your spirit according to God's choice of communication to you. Many people do not enjoy this gift because they are always in a hurry praying in tongues e

ven though God gives them the burden of the Spirit. Therefore, do not pray in tongues and stop before any of the signals come to you. It would be a waste of time. Pray until you get a breakthrough signal.

PRAY IN TONGUES TO GET TO GOD'S THRONE SIGNAL!

Remember these feedbacks from God, such as;

Seeing a vision, *joy in the heart, laughter, seeing light, a song coming out as you are praying in tongues*, *interpretation of tongues, same repeated dream, receiving voice or word of knowledge, having velvet feeling in your heart still voice in your spirit, very …… audible clear voice within your or outside directing you the way to come at of a fix.*

You can use this feedback method to pray against any disease, or plague or open any barren womb, or any problem. God uses this feedback method of the spirit as a love gift to direct you on how to achieve access and get answers from Him. That is why it is written that true worshippers shall worship God in Spirit, in John 4. You can do it, my beloved! You can do it to have a breakthrough in Jesus' Name. Keep on praying until you get it.

I have used this feedback method to get some great directions with victories from above. You will enjoy it with no regrets.

Remember this very seriously because you will never regret praying in tongues. You will tremendously benefit from it. Healing to your body will easily be established and you can live to enjoy what many people are not enjoying. God gives foolish gifts to His sons and daughters for a serious reason to shame the wise and the learned and to exalt the lowly in spirit.

Once you receive any of these feedback signs, then you know that the Holy Spirit has finished discussing with God the Father and the answer has now come and you begin blessing God for it, until you physically get it in person. Be filled with the Holy Spirit now in Jesus' Mighty Name.

AVOID THE SPIRITUAL BLOCKS

1. Unforgiveness –

2. Sinful and non-repentant life

3. Pride

4. Worries -

The truth shall set you free and free indeed.

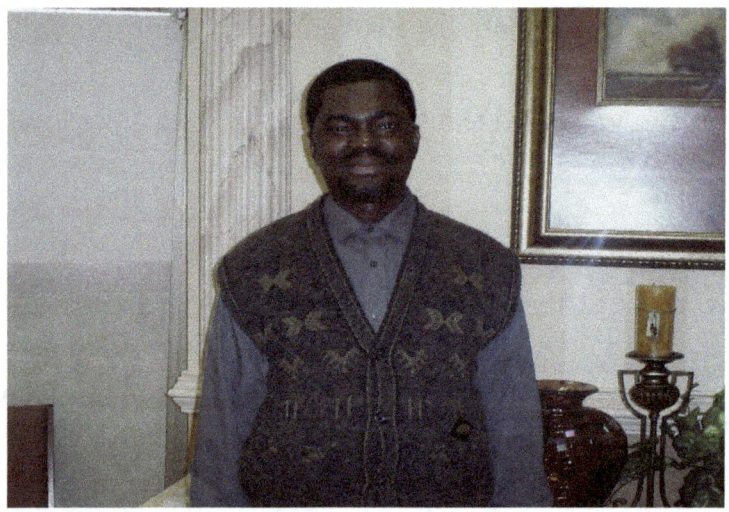

Archbishop Dr Mark Kambalazaza is the Founder of Charismatic Redeemed Ministries. God led him to found the ministry in 1998 and registered with the Government of Malawi in 2000. He is a former Roman Catholic Priest who hated and despised all born again especially those who prayed in tongues. However, the same he is writing in this book.

He officially resigned as a Catholic priest, under the advice and direction of the late Bishop Alessandro Assolari of Mangochi Diocese in 2002. He is married, to his lovely wife, Pastor Irene. They now have two children. He is an evangelist and an apostle for Christ Jesus and he has traveled in many places and nations, conducting crusades as well as being a conference speaker. His prayer is that God should use him to fulfill his God-given potential. For one day, he will stand before God to give an account of all that he did. Join him in that prayer. Then remain blessed by God and enjoy your God-given potential!

Charismatic Redeemed Ministries,

P.O. Box 1203.

BLANTYRE.

MALAWI.

Cell (+265-8201410, +265999521910)

mkambalalzaza@gmail.com

www.ingramcontent.com/pod-product-compliance
Lightning Source LLC
Chambersburg PA
CBHW062116220526
45471CB00010B/3754